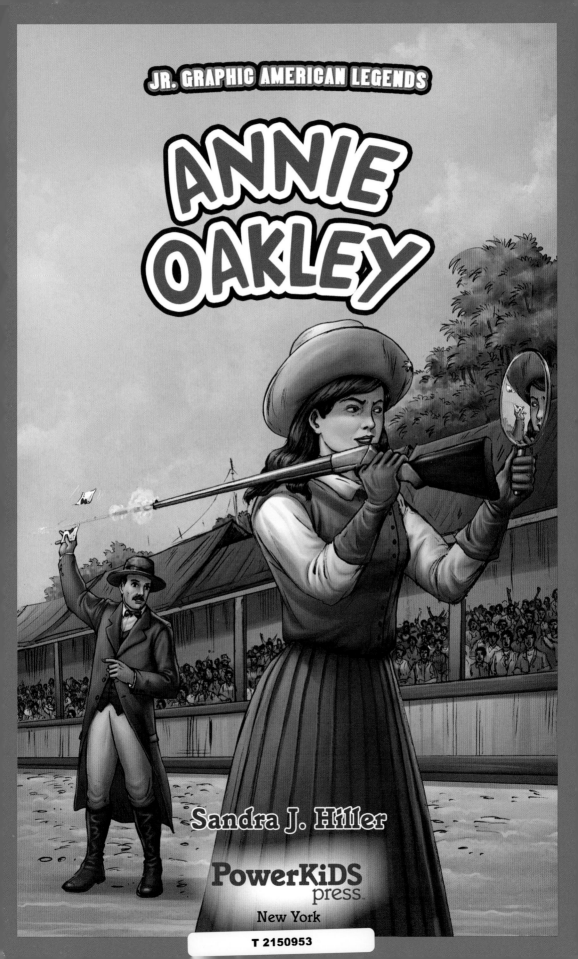

JR. GRAPHIC AMERICAN LEGENDS

ANNIE OAKLEY

Sandra J. Hiller

PowerKiDS
press.

New York

Published in 2015 by The Rosen Publishing Group, Inc.
29 East 21st Street, New York, NY 10010

First Edition

Editor: Joanne Randolph
Book Design: Contentra Technologies
Illustrations: Contentra Technologies

Library of Congress Cataloging-in-Publication Data

Hiller, Sandra J., 1956-
 Annie Oakley / by Sandra J. Hiller.
     pages cm.
 ISBN 978-1-4777-7185-3 (library binding) — ISBN 978-1-4777-7186-0 (pbk.) —
 ISBN 978-1-4777-7187-7 (6-pack)
 1. Oakley, Annie, 1860-1926—Juvenile literature. 2. Shooters of firearms—
United States—Biography—Juvenile literature. 3. Entertainers—United States—
Biography—Juvenile literature. I. Title.
 GV1157.O3H55 2015
 799.3092—dc23
 [B]
                                    2013049382

Manufactured in the United States of America
CPSIA Compliance Information: Batch #WS14PK2: For Further Information contact Rosen Publishing, New York,
New York at 1-800-237-9932

Contents

Introduction

Annie Oakley was a living, historical figure, but she became a legend, too. This makes it difficult to tell which stories about her are true and which were **fabricated** as she became famous. Her incredible skill with rifle, pistol, and shotgun were not mere legend. She could shoot accurately while riding a horse or a bicycle. She could shoot right-handed, left-handed, with the gun upside down or backward, and she rarely missed a shot. She worked hard, taking part in competitions wherever she traveled. Annie grew up in a very poor family and had little formal schooling. This made her very generous in her gifts to hospitals, orphans, and poor women wanting an education. She was a **sharpshooter**, a marksman, a performer, a gracious, generous lady, and an American legend.

Main Characters

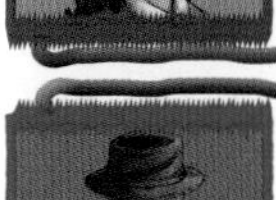

Annie Oakley (August 13, 1860–November 3, 1926) Sharpshooter and American legend.

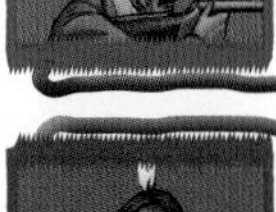

Frank Butler (February 25, 1852–November 21, 1926) Traveling marksman, performer in **variety shows**, and manager and husband of Annie Oakley.

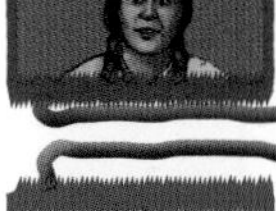

Sitting Bull (c. 1831–December 15, 1890) Hunkpapa Lakota Sioux chief and **holy man** who participated in the Battle of the Little Bighorn.

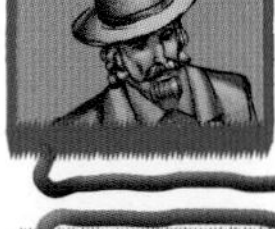

Buffalo Bill Cody (February 26, 1846–January 10, 1917) Wrangler, Pony Express rider, **cavalry scout**, and hunter who shot buffalo to feed railroad construction crews. He was the creator of the Buffalo Bill's Wild West show.

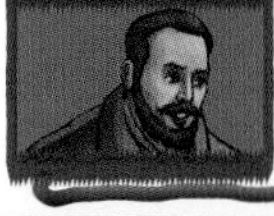

Nate Salsbury (1846–1902) Producer and manager of Buffalo Bill's Wild West show.

ANNIE OAKLEY

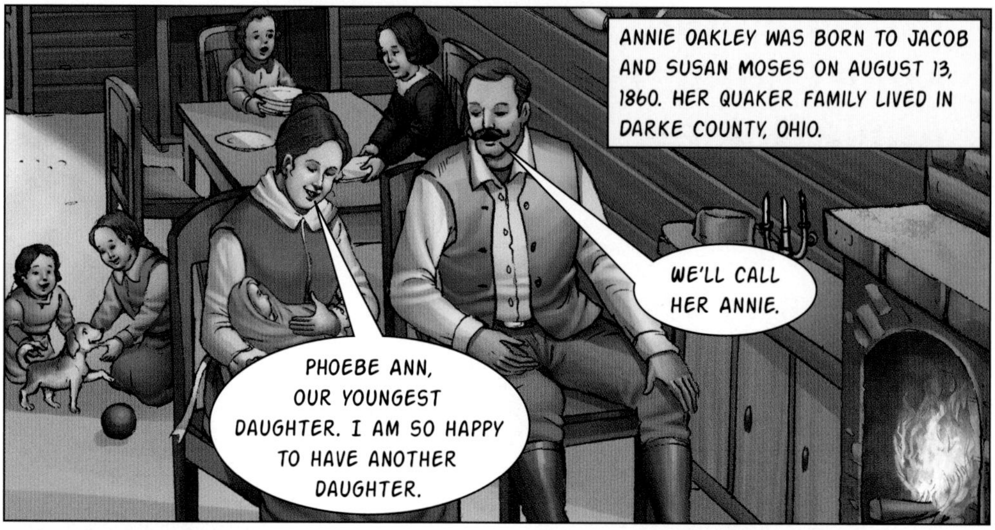
ANNIE OAKLEY WAS BORN TO JACOB AND SUSAN MOSES ON AUGUST 13, 1860. HER QUAKER FAMILY LIVED IN DARKE COUNTY, OHIO.
PHOEBE ANN, OUR YOUNGEST DAUGHTER. I AM SO HAPPY TO HAVE ANOTHER DAUGHTER.
WE'LL CALL HER ANNIE.

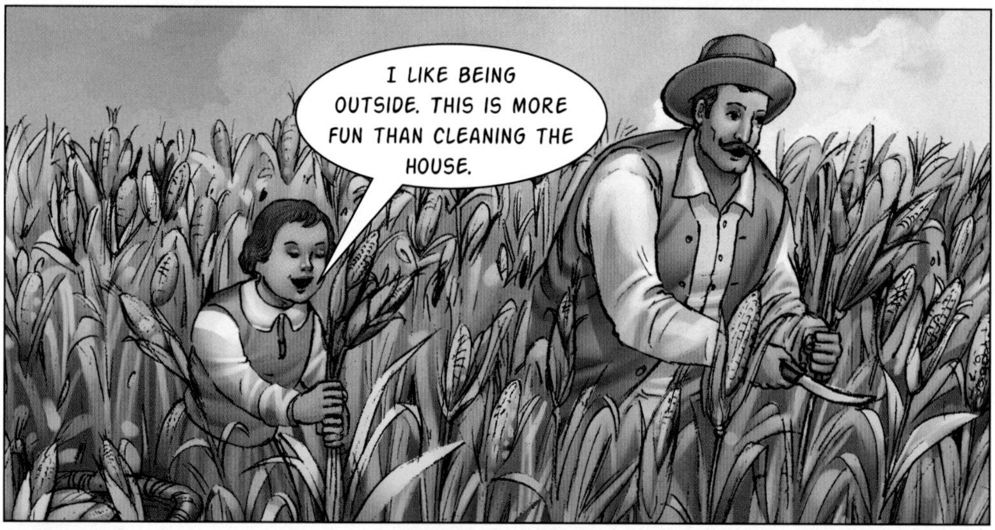
I LIKE BEING OUTSIDE. THIS IS MORE FUN THAN CLEANING THE HOUSE.

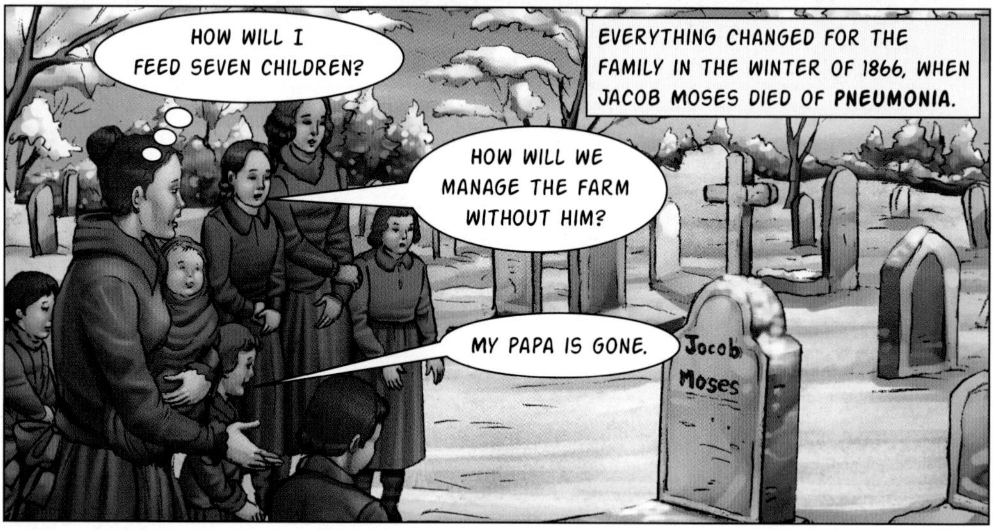
EVERYTHING CHANGED FOR THE FAMILY IN THE WINTER OF 1866, WHEN JACOB MOSES DIED OF **PNEUMONIA**.
HOW WILL I FEED SEVEN CHILDREN?
HOW WILL WE MANAGE THE FARM WITHOUT HIM?
MY PAPA IS GONE.
Jacob Moses

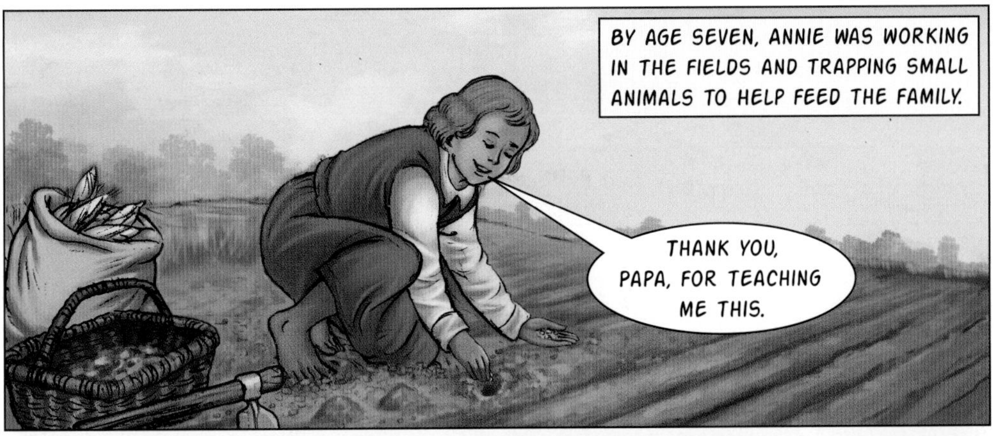
BY AGE SEVEN, ANNIE WAS WORKING IN THE FIELDS AND TRAPPING SMALL ANIMALS TO HELP FEED THE FAMILY.
THANK YOU, PAPA, FOR TEACHING ME THIS.

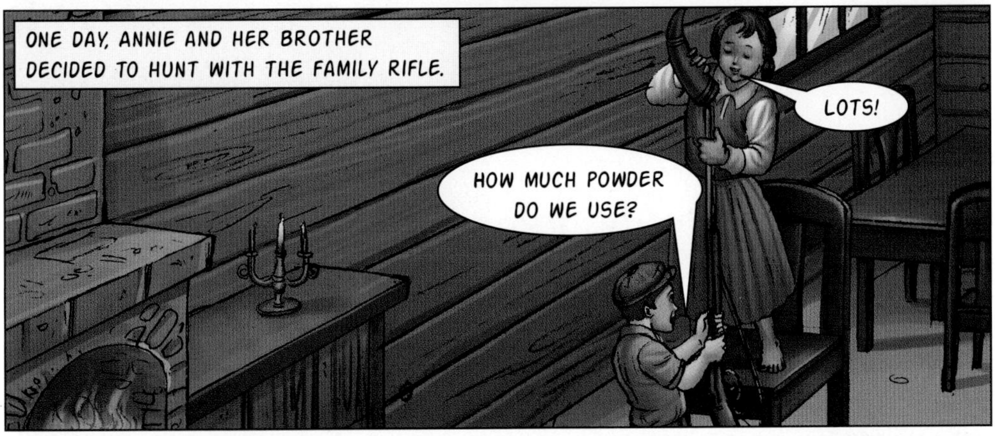
ONE DAY, ANNIE AND HER BROTHER DECIDED TO HUNT WITH THE FAMILY RIFLE.
HOW MUCH POWDER DO WE USE?
LOTS!

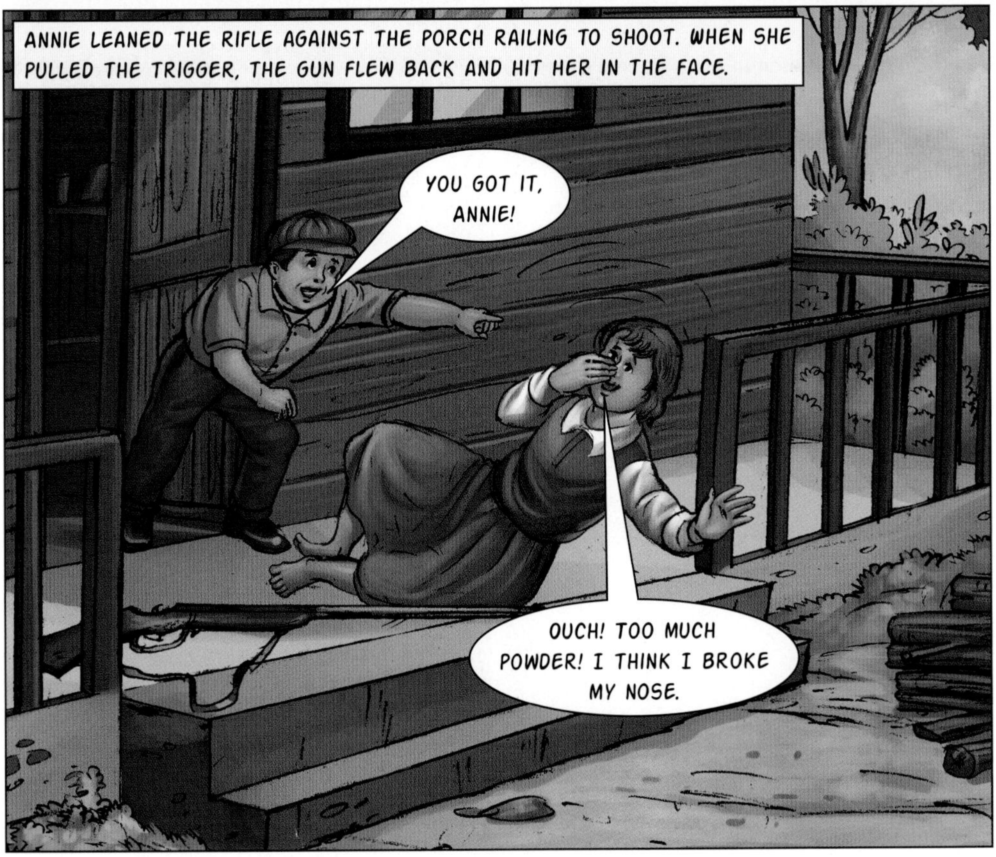
ANNIE LEANED THE RIFLE AGAINST THE PORCH RAILING TO SHOOT. WHEN SHE PULLED THE TRIGGER, THE GUN FLEW BACK AND HIT HER IN THE FACE.
YOU GOT IT, ANNIE!
OUCH! TOO MUCH POWDER! I THINK I BROKE MY NOSE.

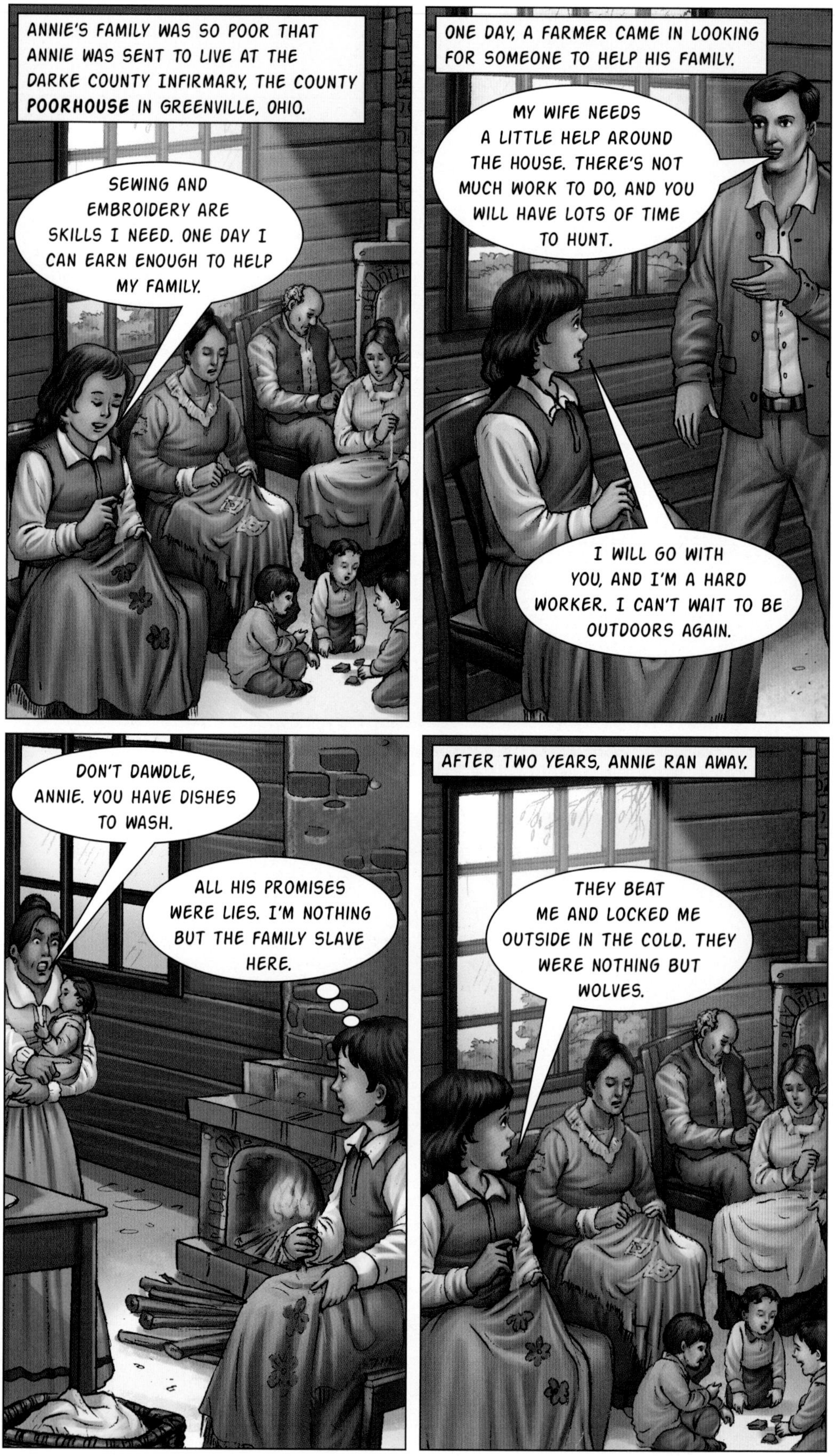
ANNIE'S FAMILY WAS SO POOR THAT ANNIE WAS SENT TO LIVE AT THE DARKE COUNTY INFIRMARY, THE COUNTY POORHOUSE IN GREENVILLE, OHIO.
SEWING AND EMBROIDERY ARE SKILLS I NEED. ONE DAY I CAN EARN ENOUGH TO HELP MY FAMILY.
ONE DAY, A FARMER CAME IN LOOKING FOR SOMEONE TO HELP HIS FAMILY.
MY WIFE NEEDS A LITTLE HELP AROUND THE HOUSE. THERE'S NOT MUCH WORK TO DO, AND YOU WILL HAVE LOTS OF TIME TO HUNT.
I WILL GO WITH YOU, AND I'M A HARD WORKER. I CAN'T WAIT TO BE OUTDOORS AGAIN.
DON'T DAWDLE, ANNIE. YOU HAVE DISHES TO WASH.
ALL HIS PROMISES WERE LIES. I'M NOTHING BUT THE FAMILY SLAVE HERE.
AFTER TWO YEARS, ANNIE RAN AWAY.
THEY BEAT ME AND LOCKED ME OUTSIDE IN THE COLD. THEY WERE NOTHING BUT WOLVES.

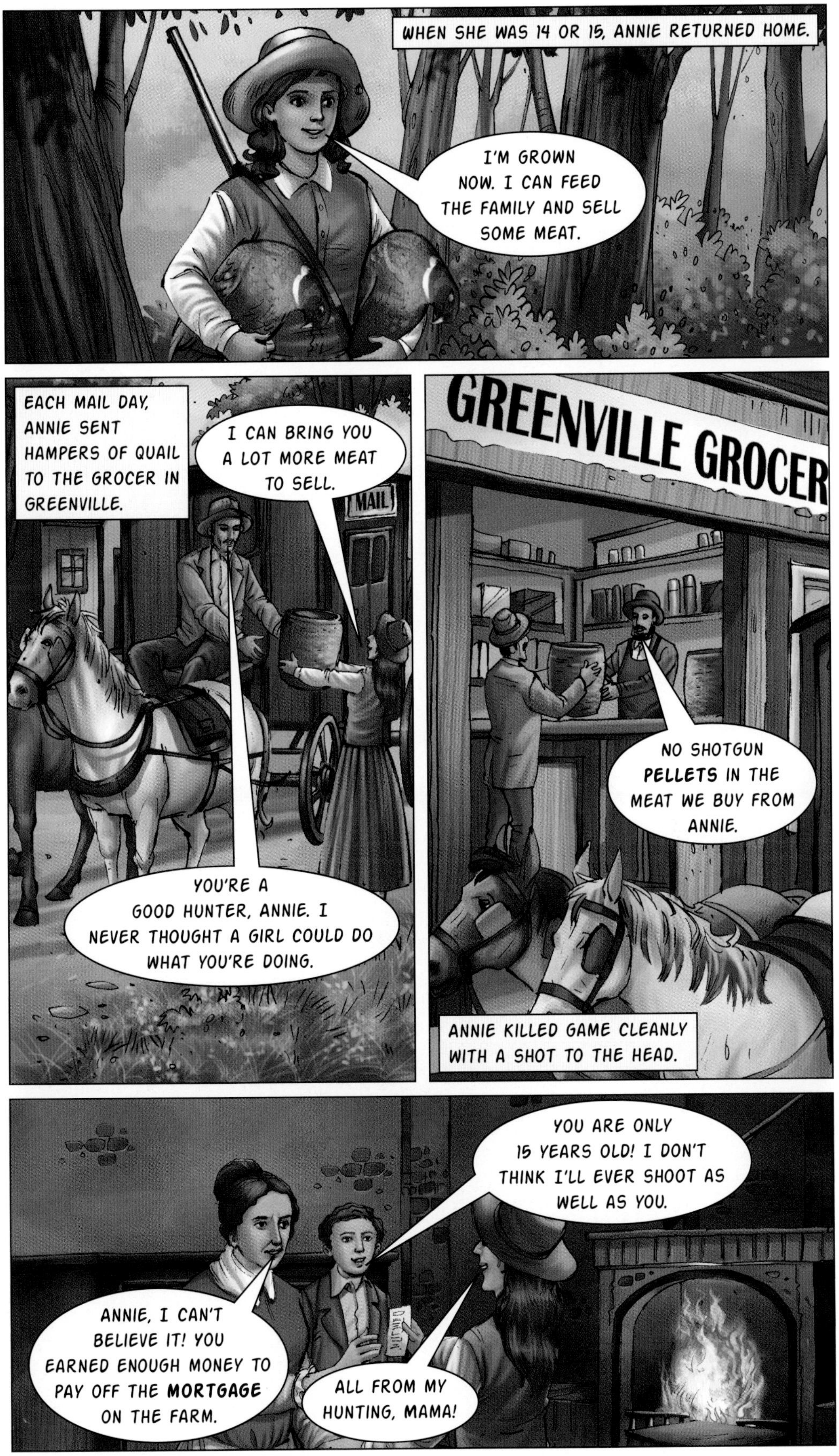
WHEN SHE WAS 14 OR 15, ANNIE RETURNED HOME.
I'M GROWN NOW. I CAN FEED THE FAMILY AND SELL SOME MEAT.
EACH MAIL DAY, ANNIE SENT HAMPERS OF QUAIL TO THE GROCER IN GREENVILLE.
I CAN BRING YOU A LOT MORE MEAT TO SELL.
MAIL
YOU'RE A GOOD HUNTER, ANNIE. I NEVER THOUGHT A GIRL COULD DO WHAT YOU'RE DOING.
GREENVILLE GROCER
NO SHOTGUN **PELLETS** IN THE MEAT WE BUY FROM ANNIE.
ANNIE KILLED GAME CLEANLY WITH A SHOT TO THE HEAD.
YOU ARE ONLY 15 YEARS OLD! I DON'T THINK I'LL EVER SHOOT AS WELL AS YOU.
ANNIE, I CAN'T BELIEVE IT! YOU EARNED ENOUGH MONEY TO PAY OFF THE **MORTGAGE** ON THE FARM.
ALL FROM MY HUNTING, MAMA!

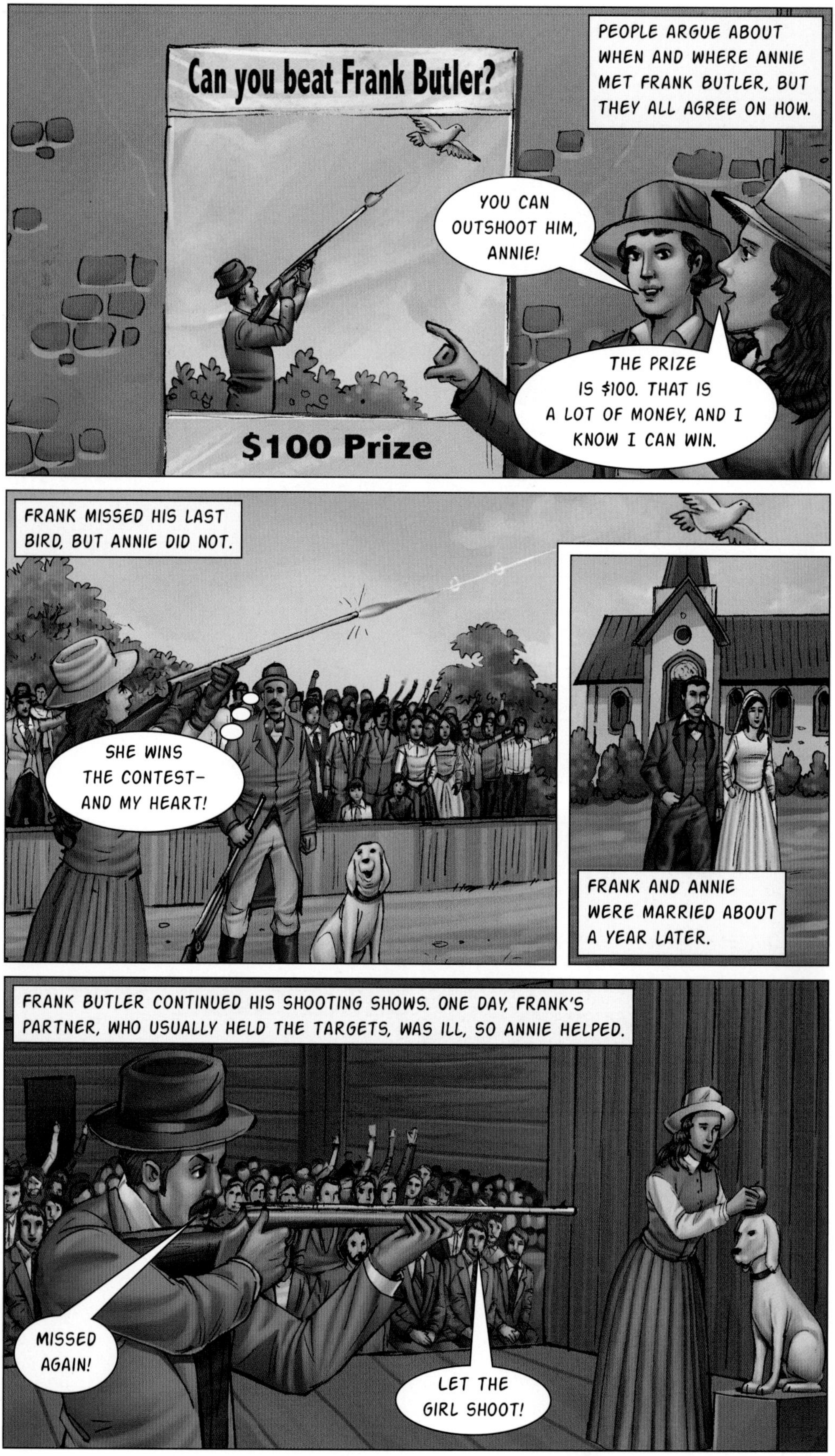
Can you beat Frank Butler?
$100 Prize
PEOPLE ARGUE ABOUT WHEN AND WHERE ANNIE MET FRANK BUTLER, BUT THEY ALL AGREE ON HOW.
YOU CAN OUTSHOOT HIM, ANNIE!
THE PRIZE IS $100. THAT IS A LOT OF MONEY, AND I KNOW I CAN WIN.
FRANK MISSED HIS LAST BIRD, BUT ANNIE DID NOT.
SHE WINS THE CONTEST— AND MY HEART!
FRANK AND ANNIE WERE MARRIED ABOUT A YEAR LATER.
FRANK BUTLER CONTINUED HIS SHOOTING SHOWS. ONE DAY, FRANK'S PARTNER, WHO USUALLY HELD THE TARGETS, WAS ILL, SO ANNIE HELPED.
MISSED AGAIN!
LET THE GIRL SHOOT!

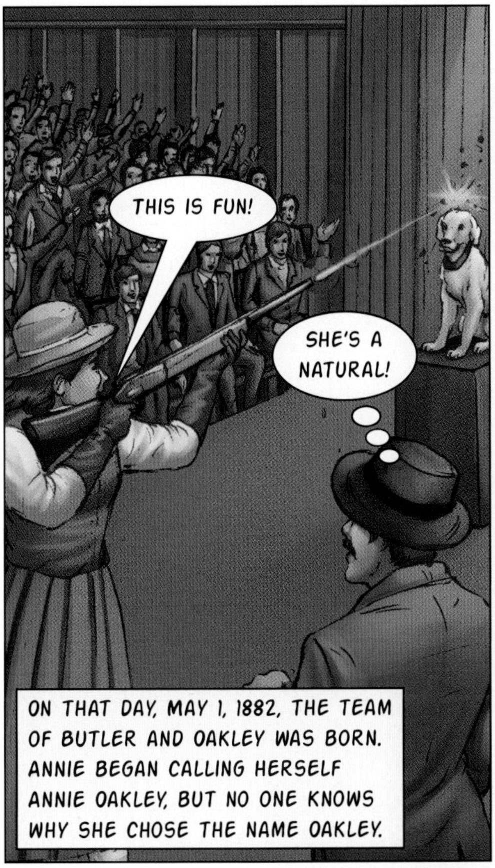
THIS IS FUN!
SHE'S A NATURAL!
ON THAT DAY, MAY 1, 1882, THE TEAM OF BUTLER AND OAKLEY WAS BORN. ANNIE BEGAN CALLING HERSELF ANNIE OAKLEY, BUT NO ONE KNOWS WHY SHE CHOSE THE NAME OAKLEY.

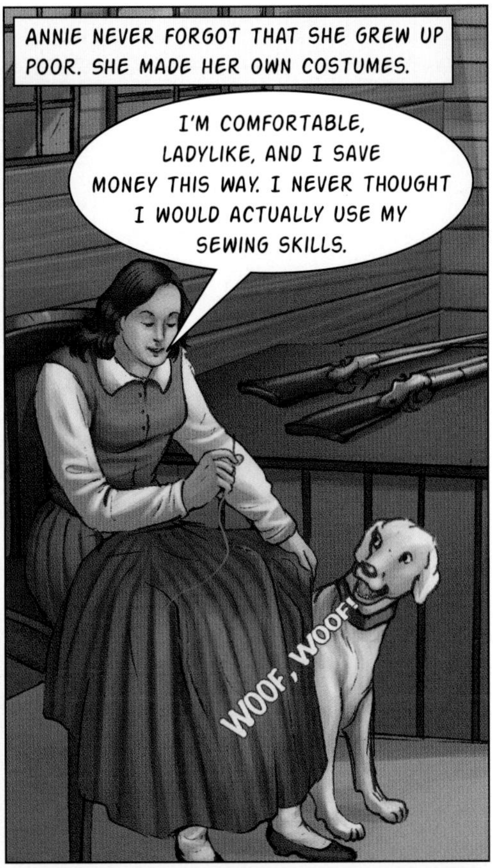
ANNIE NEVER FORGOT THAT SHE GREW UP POOR. SHE MADE HER OWN COSTUMES.
I'M COMFORTABLE, LADYLIKE, AND I SAVE MONEY THIS WAY. I NEVER THOUGHT I WOULD ACTUALLY USE MY SEWING SKILLS.
WOOF, WOOF!

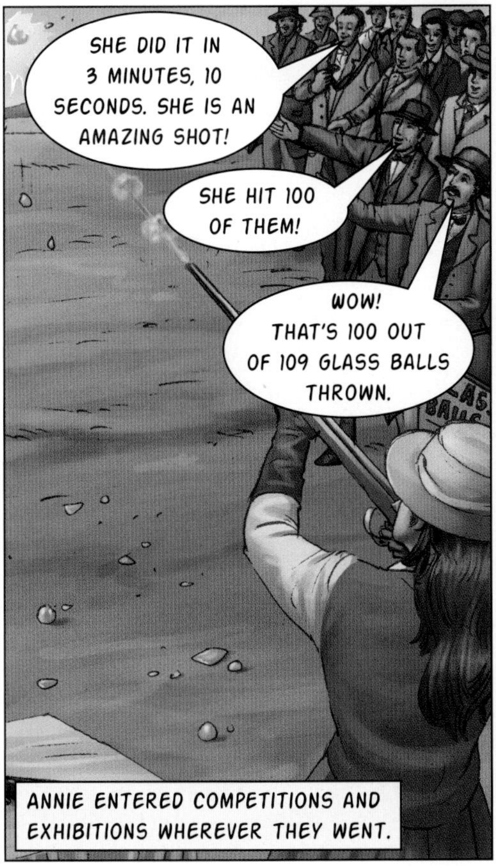
SHE DID IT IN 3 MINUTES, 10 SECONDS. SHE IS AN AMAZING SHOT!
SHE HIT 100 OF THEM!
WOW! THAT'S 100 OUT OF 109 GLASS BALLS THROWN.
ANNIE ENTERED COMPETITIONS AND EXHIBITIONS WHEREVER THEY WENT.

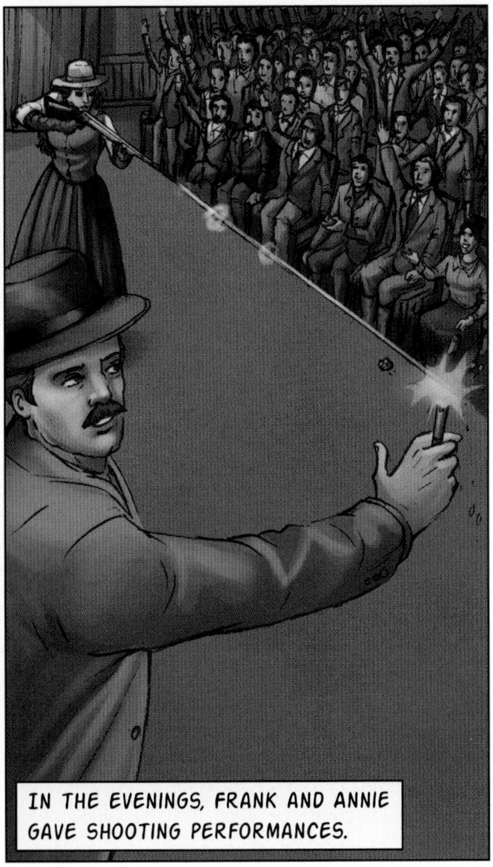
IN THE EVENINGS, FRANK AND ANNIE GAVE SHOOTING PERFORMANCES.

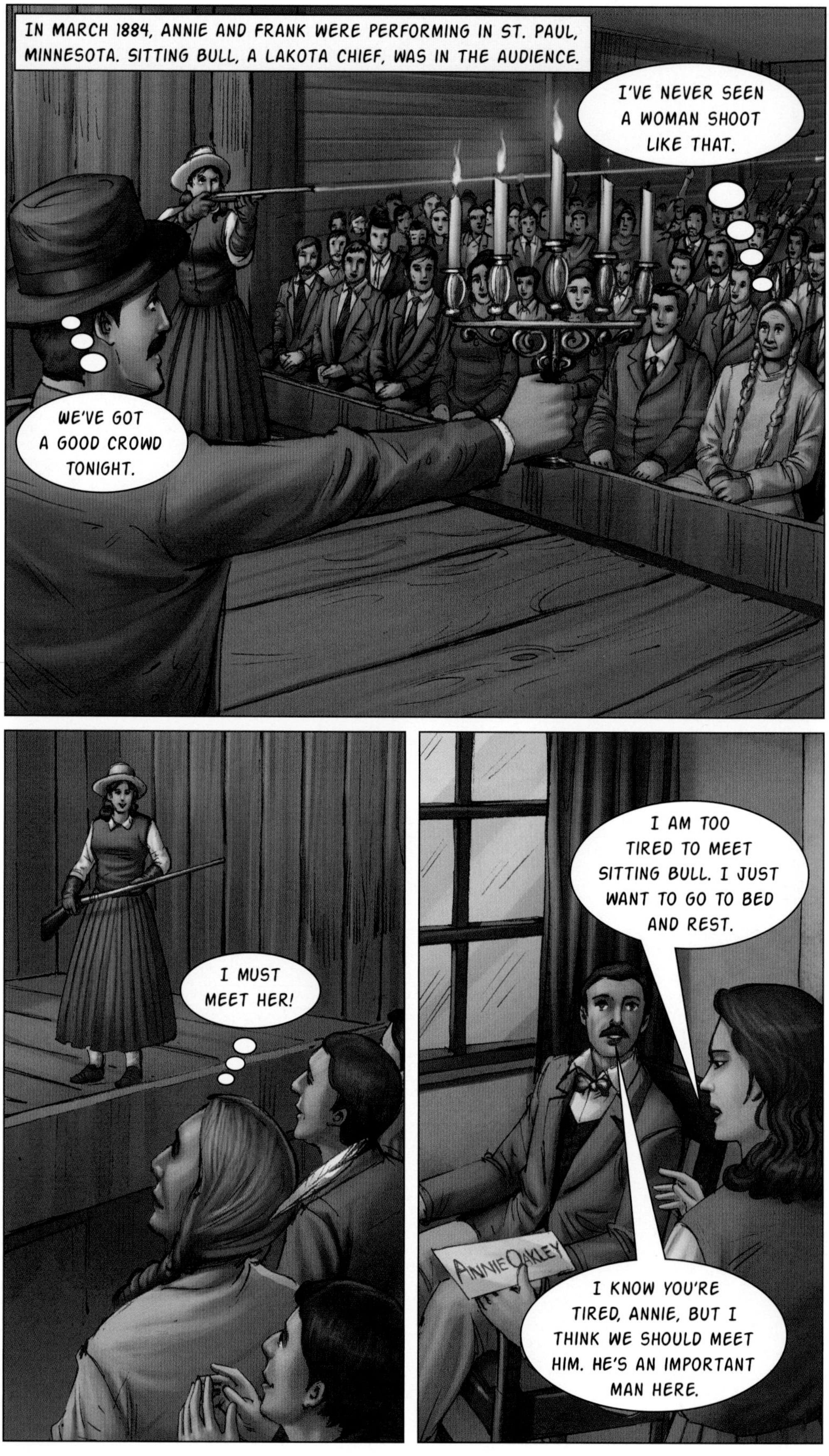

IN MARCH 1884, ANNIE AND FRANK WERE PERFORMING IN ST. PAUL, MINNESOTA. SITTING BULL, A LAKOTA CHIEF, WAS IN THE AUDIENCE.
WE'VE GOT A GOOD CROWD TONIGHT.
I'VE NEVER SEEN A WOMAN SHOOT LIKE THAT.
I MUST MEET HER!
I AM TOO TIRED TO MEET SITTING BULL. I JUST WANT TO GO TO BED AND REST.
ANNIE OAKLEY
I KNOW YOU'RE TIRED, ANNIE, BUT I THINK WE SHOULD MEET HIM. HE'S AN IMPORTANT MAN HERE.

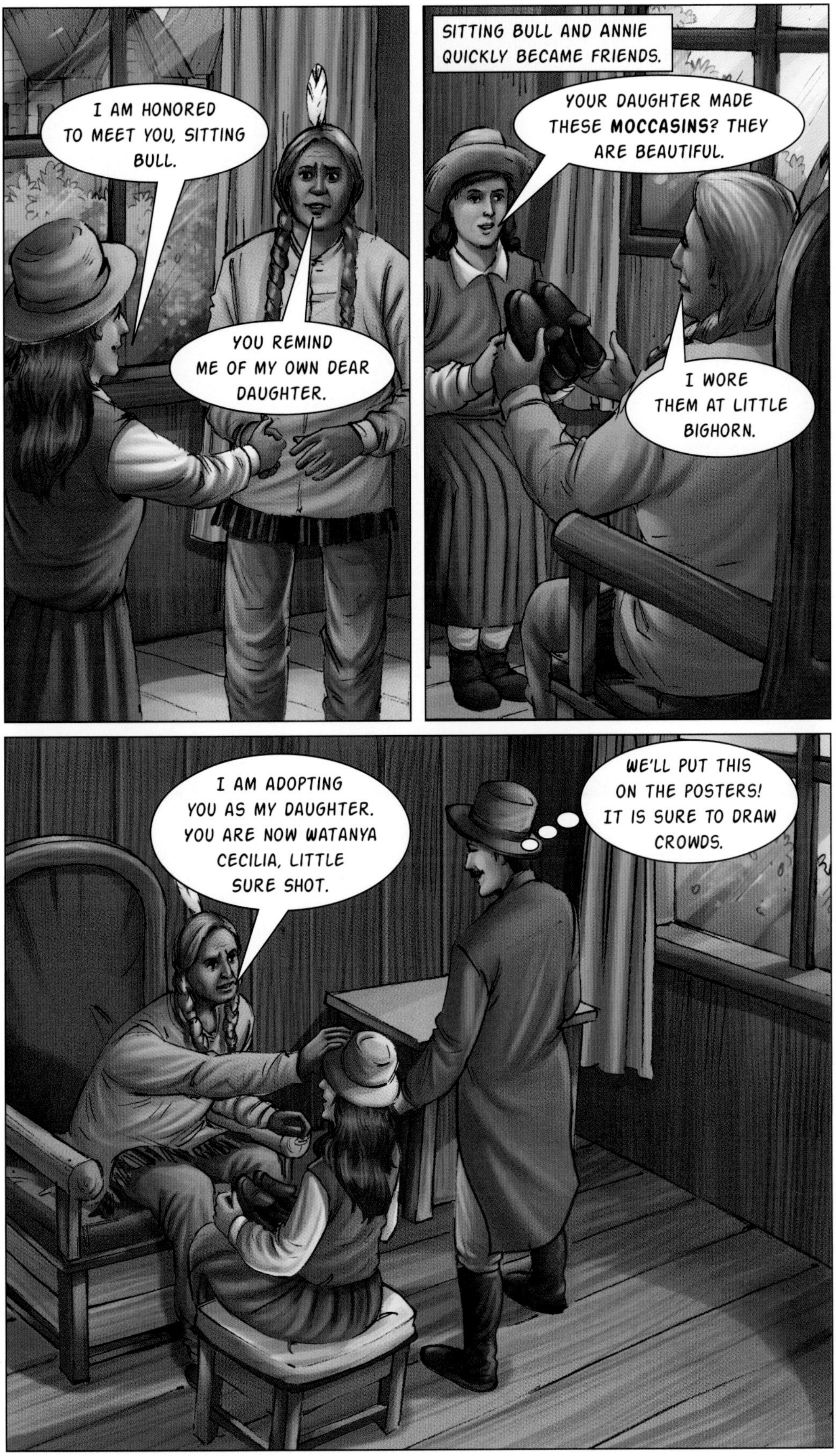
I AM HONORED TO MEET YOU, SITTING BULL.
YOU REMIND ME OF MY OWN DEAR DAUGHTER.
SITTING BULL AND ANNIE QUICKLY BECAME FRIENDS.
YOUR DAUGHTER MADE THESE **MOCCASINS**? THEY ARE BEAUTIFUL.
I WORE THEM AT LITTLE BIGHORN.
I AM ADOPTING YOU AS MY DAUGHTER. YOU ARE NOW WATANYA CECILIA, LITTLE SURE SHOT.
WE'LL PUT THIS ON THE POSTERS! IT IS SURE TO DRAW CROWDS.

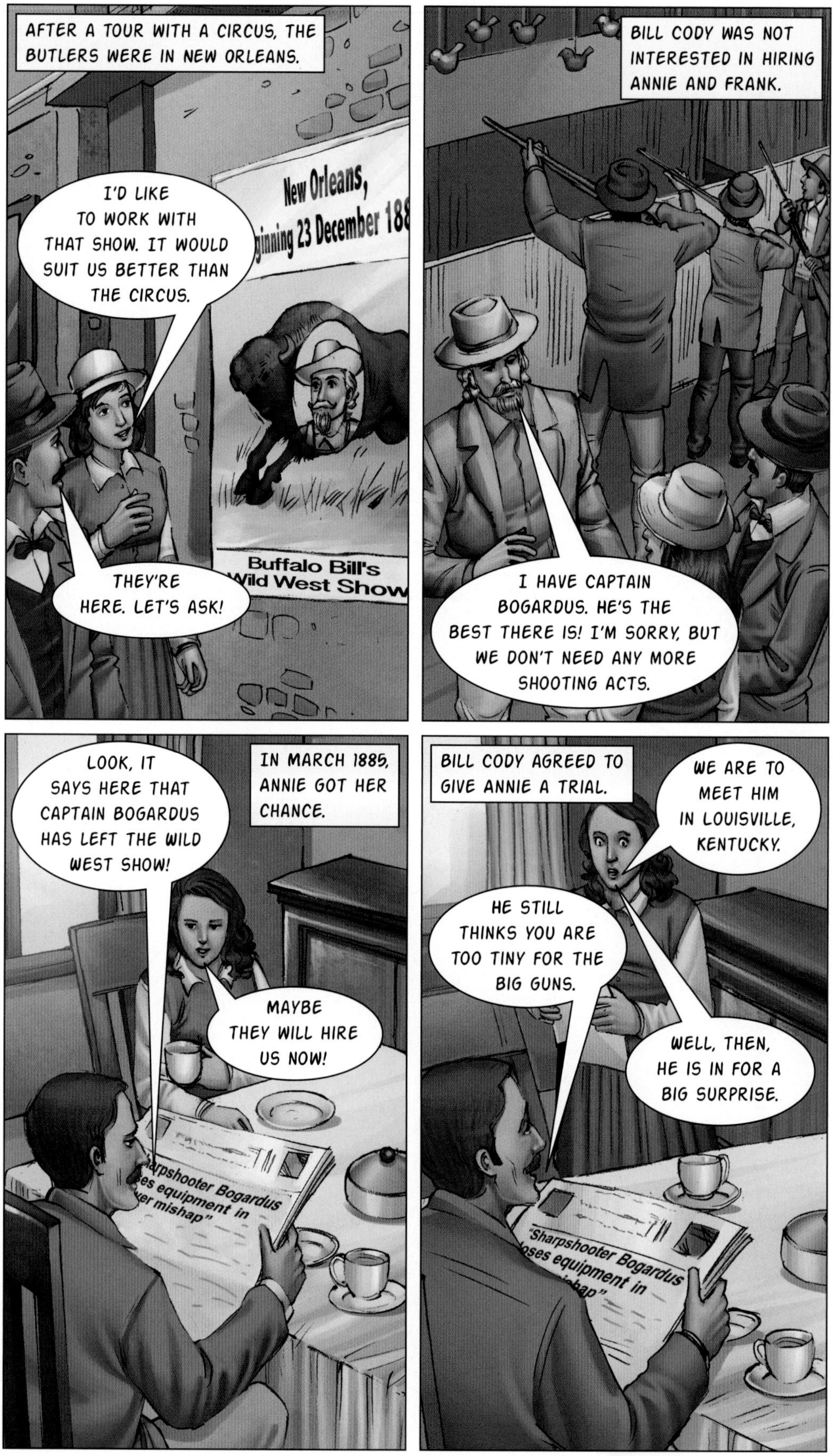
AFTER A TOUR WITH A CIRCUS, THE BUTLERS WERE IN NEW ORLEANS.
I'D LIKE TO WORK WITH THAT SHOW. IT WOULD SUIT US BETTER THAN THE CIRCUS.
New Orleans,
Buffalo Bill's
THEY'RE HERE. LET'S ASK!
BILL CODY WAS NOT INTERESTED IN HIRING ANNIE AND FRANK.
I HAVE CAPTAIN BOGARDUS. HE'S THE BEST THERE IS! I'M SORRY, BUT WE DON'T NEED ANY MORE SHOOTING ACTS.
IN MARCH 1885, ANNIE GOT HER CHANCE.
LOOK, IT SAYS HERE THAT CAPTAIN BOGARDUS HAS LEFT THE WILD WEST SHOW!
MAYBE THEY WILL HIRE US NOW!
BILL CODY AGREED TO GIVE ANNIE A TRIAL.
WE ARE TO MEET HIM IN LOUISVILLE, KENTUCKY.
HE STILL THINKS YOU ARE TOO TINY FOR THE BIG GUNS.
WELL, THEN, HE IS IN FOR A BIG SURPRISE.
"Sharpshooter Bogardus

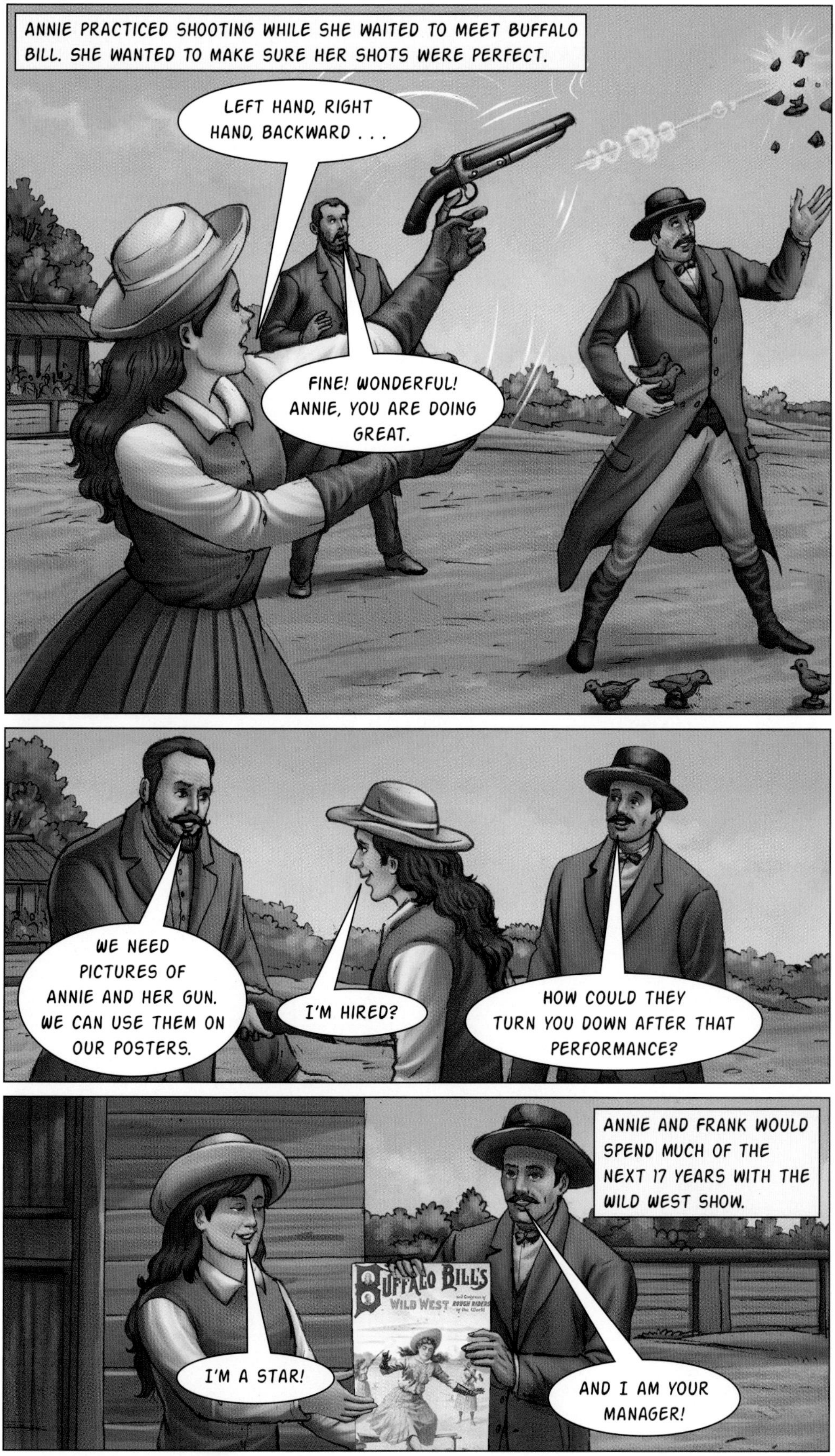
ANNIE PRACTICED SHOOTING WHILE SHE WAITED TO MEET BUFFALO BILL. SHE WANTED TO MAKE SURE HER SHOTS WERE PERFECT.
LEFT HAND, RIGHT HAND, BACKWARD . . .
FINE! WONDERFUL! ANNIE, YOU ARE DOING GREAT.
WE NEED PICTURES OF ANNIE AND HER GUN. WE CAN USE THEM ON OUR POSTERS.
I'M HIRED?
HOW COULD THEY TURN YOU DOWN AFTER THAT PERFORMANCE?
ANNIE AND FRANK WOULD SPEND MUCH OF THE NEXT 17 YEARS WITH THE WILD WEST SHOW.
BUFFALO BILL'S
WILD WEST
ROUGH RIDERS
I'M A STAR!
AND I AM YOUR MANAGER!

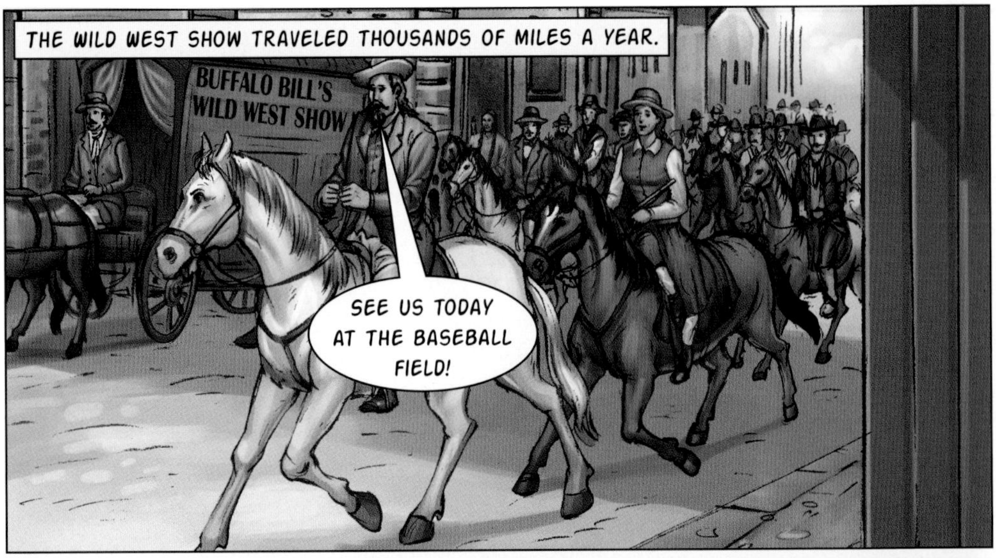
THE WILD WEST SHOW TRAVELED THOUSANDS OF MILES A YEAR.
BUFFALO BILL'S WILD WEST SHOW
SEE US TODAY AT THE BASEBALL FIELD!

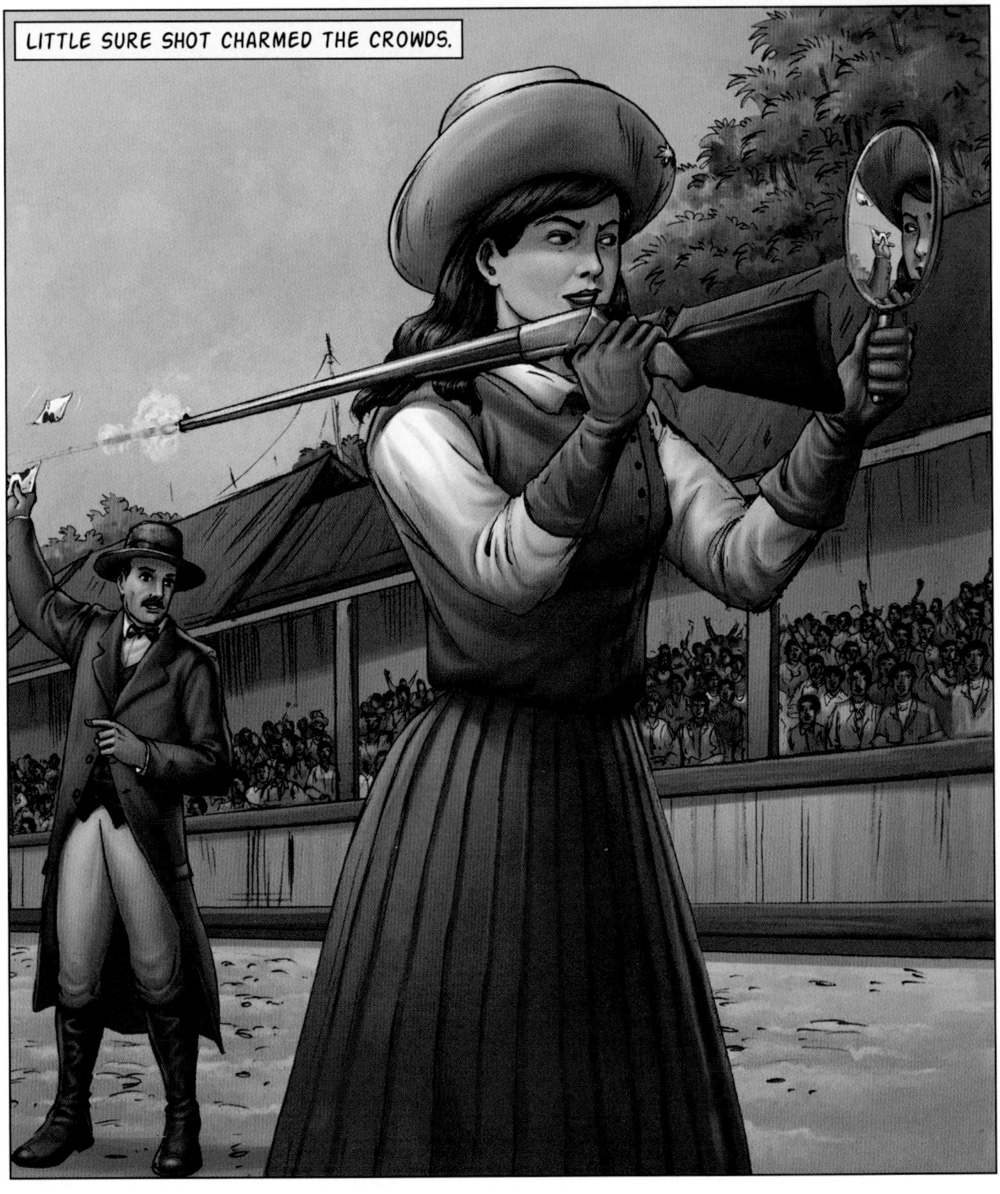
LITTLE SURE SHOT CHARMED THE CROWDS.

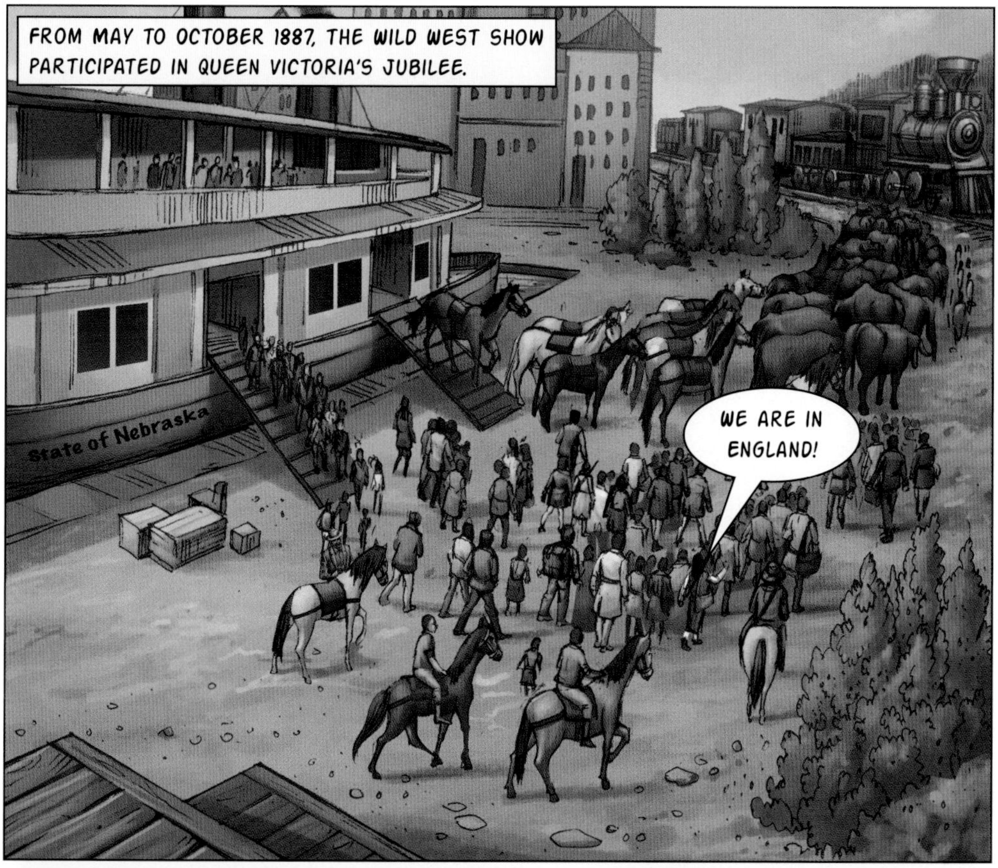
FROM MAY TO OCTOBER 1887, THE WILD WEST SHOW PARTICIPATED IN QUEEN VICTORIA'S JUBILEE.
State of Nebraska
WE ARE IN ENGLAND!

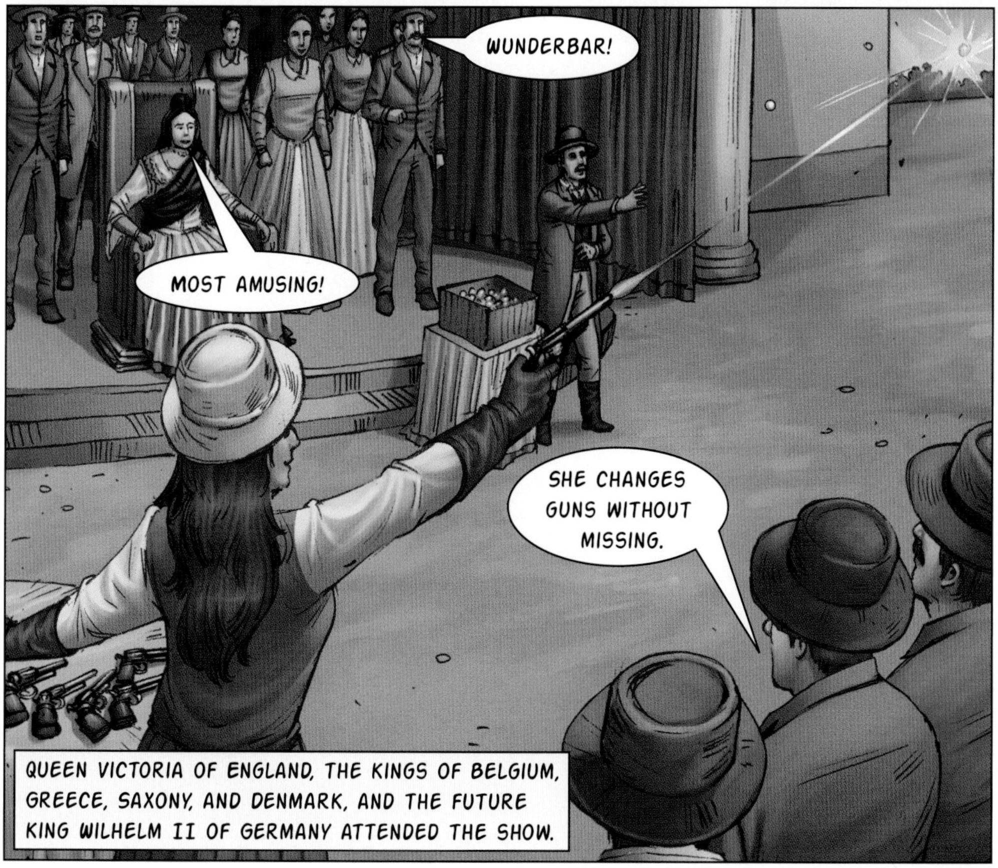
WUNDERBAR!
MOST AMUSING!
SHE CHANGES GUNS WITHOUT MISSING.
QUEEN VICTORIA OF ENGLAND, THE KINGS OF BELGIUM, GREECE, SAXONY, AND DENMARK, AND THE FUTURE KING WILHELM II OF GERMANY ATTENDED THE SHOW.

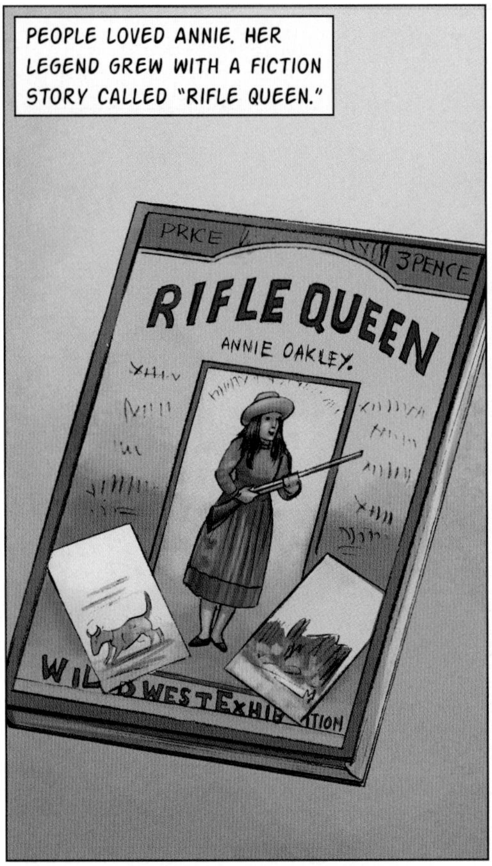
PEOPLE LOVED ANNIE. HER LEGEND GREW WITH A FICTION STORY CALLED "RIFLE QUEEN."
PRICE
3PENCE
RIFLE QUEEN
ANNIE OAKLEY.
WILD WEST EXHIBITION

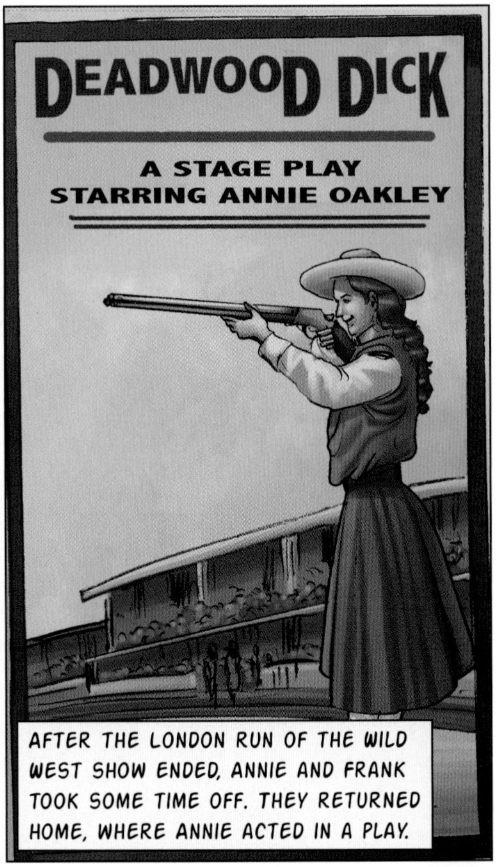
DEADWOOD DICK
A STAGE PLAY
STARRING ANNIE OAKLEY
AFTER THE LONDON RUN OF THE WILD WEST SHOW ENDED, ANNIE AND FRANK TOOK SOME TIME OFF. THEY RETURNED HOME, WHERE ANNIE ACTED IN A PLAY.

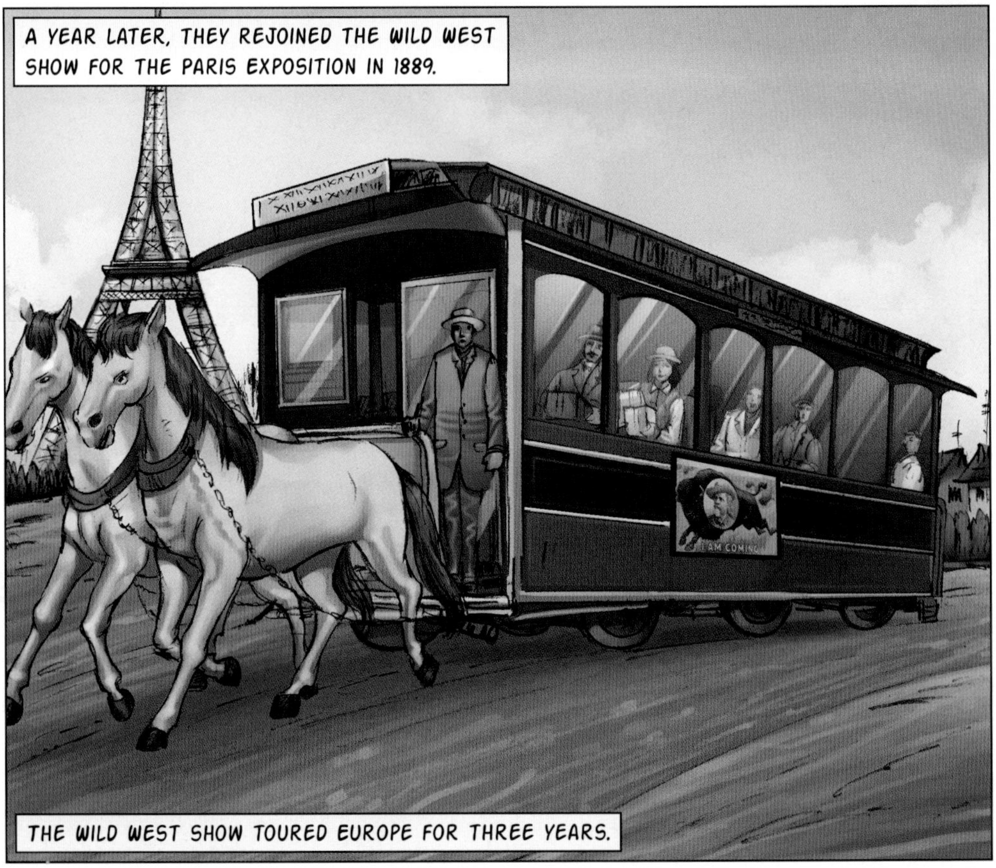
A YEAR LATER, THEY REJOINED THE WILD WEST SHOW FOR THE PARIS EXPOSITION IN 1889.
I AM COMING
THE WILD WEST SHOW TOURED EUROPE FOR THREE YEARS.

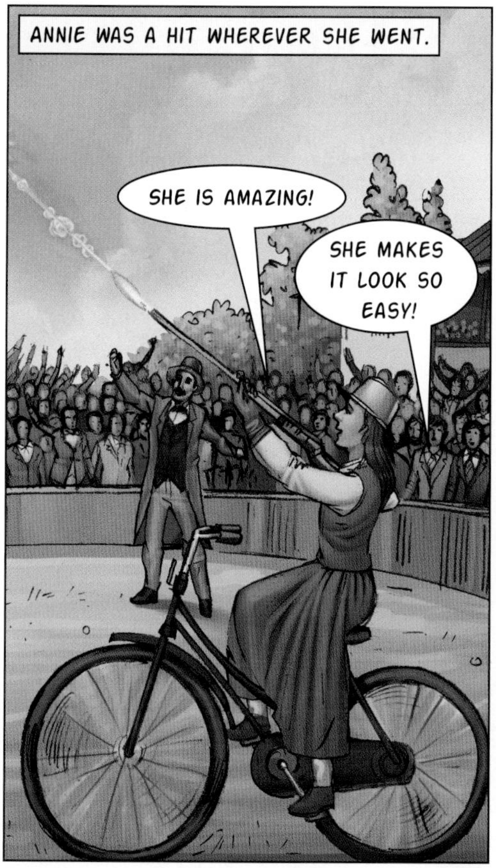
ANNIE WAS A HIT WHEREVER SHE WENT.
SHE IS AMAZING!
SHE MAKES IT LOOK SO EASY!

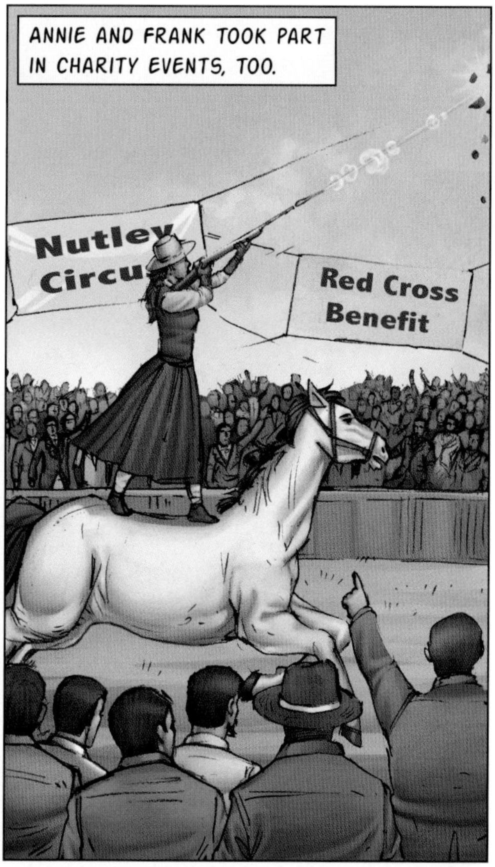
ANNIE AND FRANK TOOK PART IN CHARITY EVENTS, TOO.
Nutley Circu
Red Cross Benefit

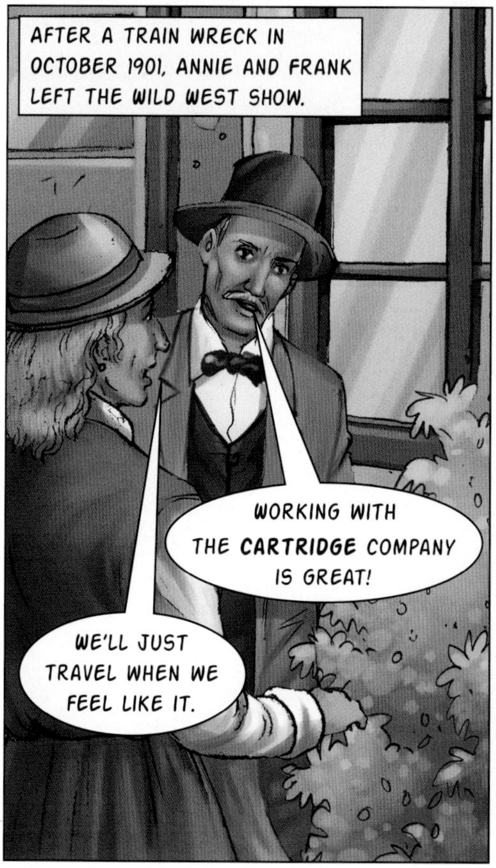
AFTER A TRAIN WRECK IN OCTOBER 1901, ANNIE AND FRANK LEFT THE WILD WEST SHOW.
WORKING WITH THE CARTRIDGE COMPANY IS GREAT!
WE'LL JUST TRAVEL WHEN WE FEEL LIKE IT.

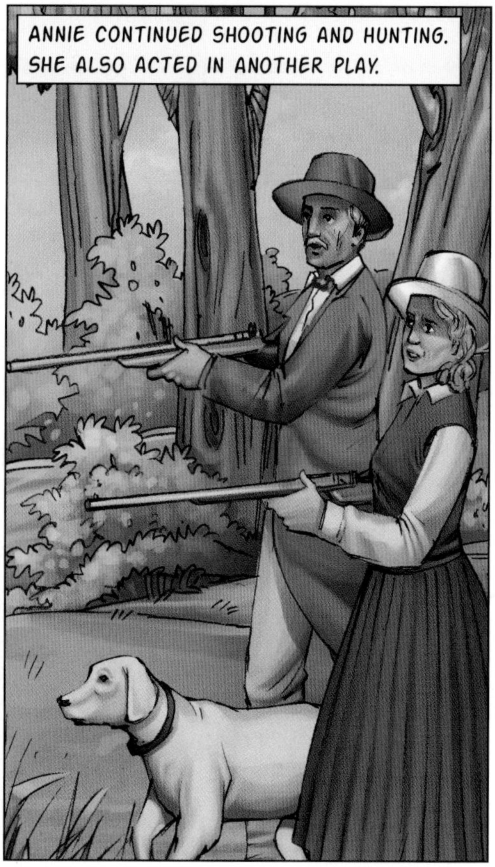
ANNIE CONTINUED SHOOTING AND HUNTING. SHE ALSO ACTED IN ANOTHER PLAY.

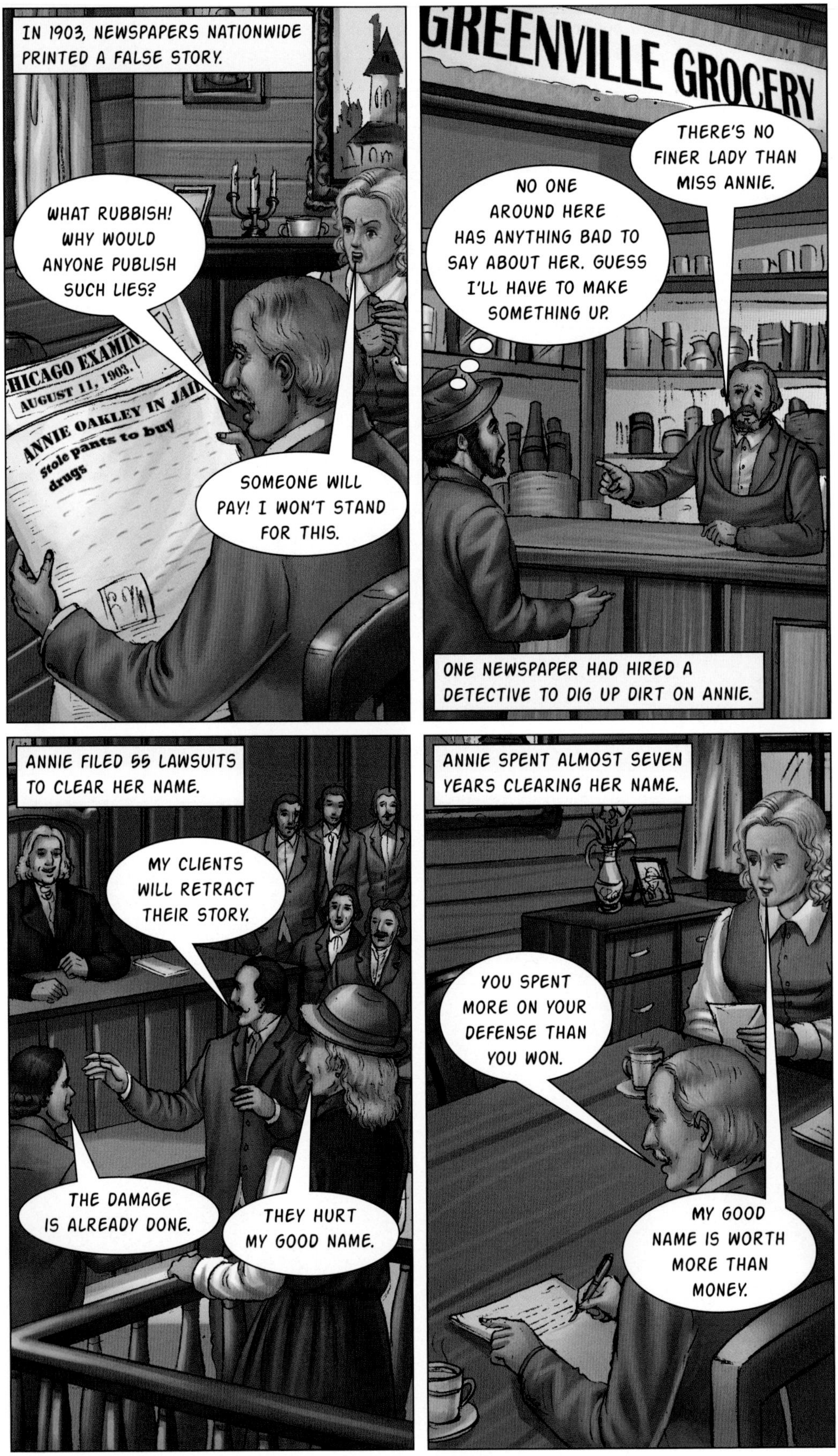
IN 1903, NEWSPAPERS NATIONWIDE PRINTED A FALSE STORY.
CHICAGO EXAMIN
AUGUST 11, 1903.
ANNIE OAKLEY IN JAI
Stole pants to buy drugs
WHAT RUBBISH! WHY WOULD ANYONE PUBLISH SUCH LIES?
SOMEONE WILL PAY! I WON'T STAND FOR THIS.
GREENVILLE GROCERY
THERE'S NO FINER LADY THAN MISS ANNIE.
NO ONE AROUND HERE HAS ANYTHING BAD TO SAY ABOUT HER. GUESS I'LL HAVE TO MAKE SOMETHING UP.
ONE NEWSPAPER HAD HIRED A DETECTIVE TO DIG UP DIRT ON ANNIE.
ANNIE FILED 55 LAWSUITS TO CLEAR HER NAME.
MY CLIENTS WILL RETRACT THEIR STORY.
THE DAMAGE IS ALREADY DONE.
THEY HURT MY GOOD NAME.
ANNIE SPENT ALMOST SEVEN YEARS CLEARING HER NAME.
YOU SPENT MORE ON YOUR DEFENSE THAN YOU WON.
MY GOOD NAME IS WORTH MORE THAN MONEY.

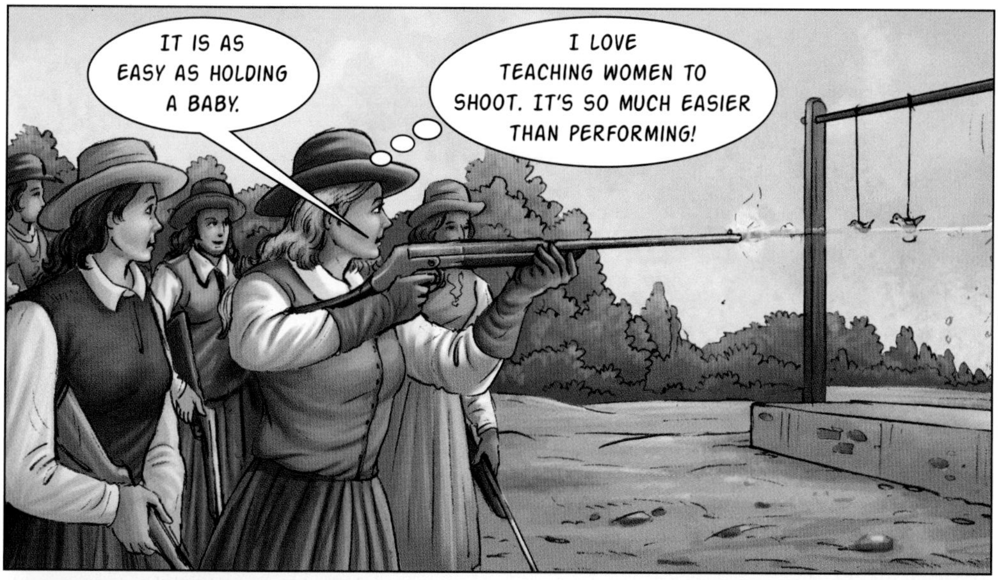
IT IS AS EASY AS HOLDING A BABY.
I LOVE TEACHING WOMEN TO SHOOT. IT'S SO MUCH EASIER THAN PERFORMING!

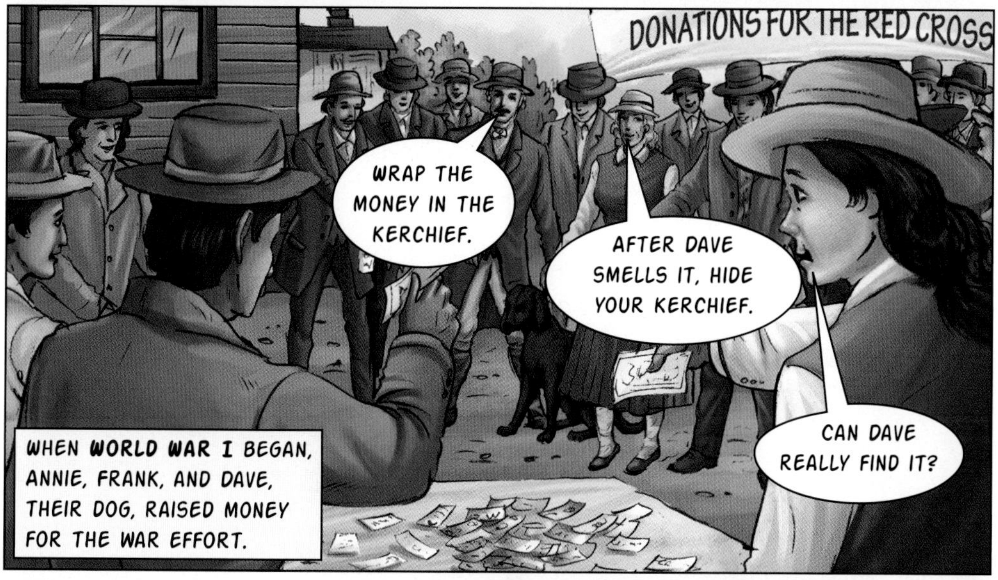
DONATIONS FOR THE RED CROSS
WRAP THE MONEY IN THE KERCHIEF.
AFTER DAVE SMELLS IT, HIDE YOUR KERCHIEF.
CAN DAVE REALLY FIND IT?
WHEN WORLD WAR I BEGAN, ANNIE, FRANK, AND DAVE, THEIR DOG, RAISED MONEY FOR THE WAR EFFORT.

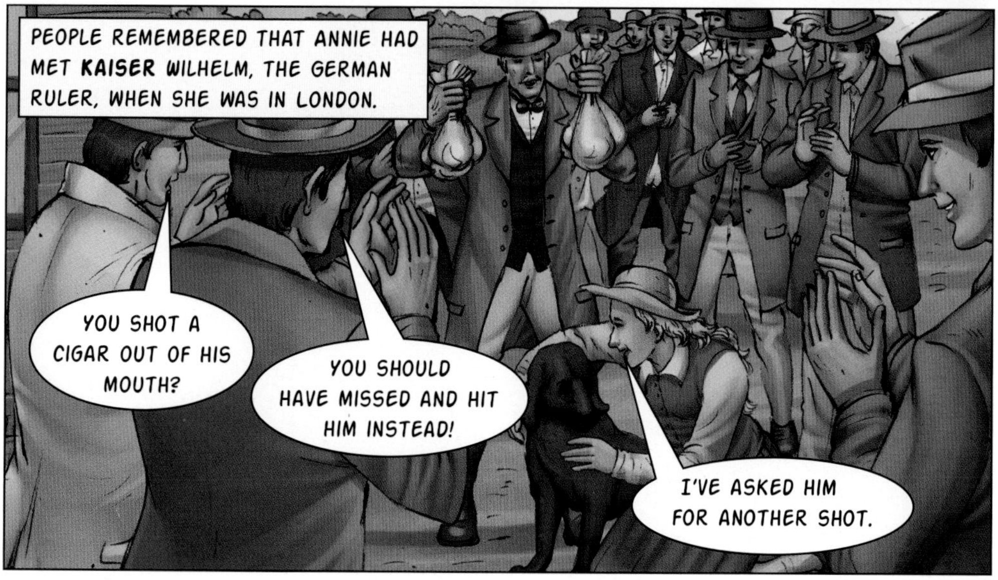
PEOPLE REMEMBERED THAT ANNIE HAD MET KAISER WILHELM, THE GERMAN RULER, WHEN SHE WAS IN LONDON.
YOU SHOT A CIGAR OUT OF HIS MOUTH?
YOU SHOULD HAVE MISSED AND HIT HIM INSTEAD!
I'VE ASKED HIM FOR ANOTHER SHOT.

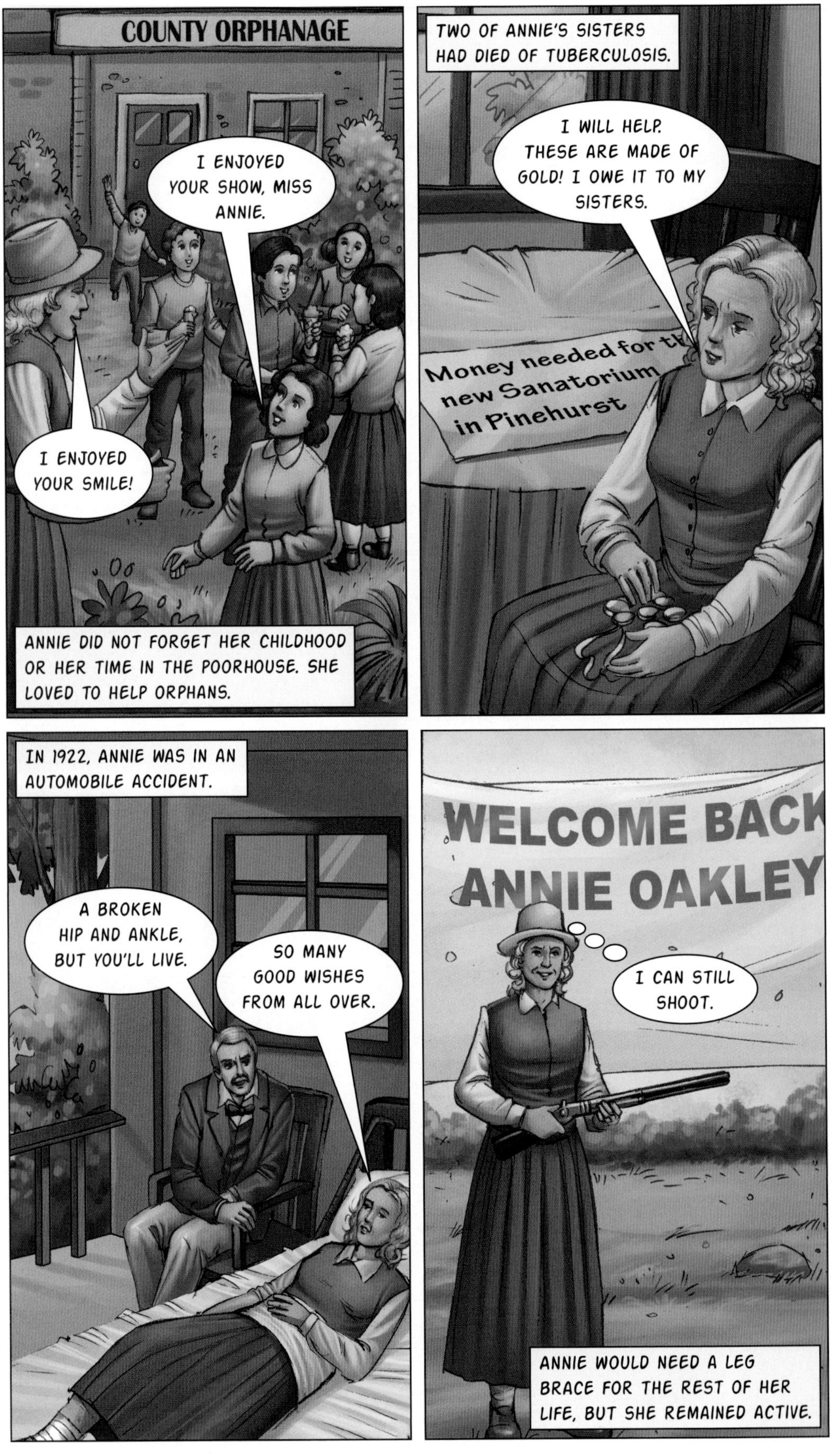
COUNTY ORPHANAGE
I ENJOYED YOUR SHOW, MISS ANNIE.
I ENJOYED YOUR SMILE!
ANNIE DID NOT FORGET HER CHILDHOOD OR HER TIME IN THE POORHOUSE. SHE LOVED TO HELP ORPHANS.
TWO OF ANNIE'S SISTERS HAD DIED OF TUBERCULOSIS.
I WILL HELP. THESE ARE MADE OF GOLD! I OWE IT TO MY SISTERS.
Money needed for th new Sanatorium in Pinehurst
IN 1922, ANNIE WAS IN AN AUTOMOBILE ACCIDENT.
A BROKEN HIP AND ANKLE, BUT YOU'LL LIVE.
SO MANY GOOD WISHES FROM ALL OVER.
WELCOME BACK ANNIE OAKLEY
I CAN STILL SHOOT.
ANNIE WOULD NEED A LEG BRACE FOR THE REST OF HER LIFE, BUT SHE REMAINED ACTIVE.

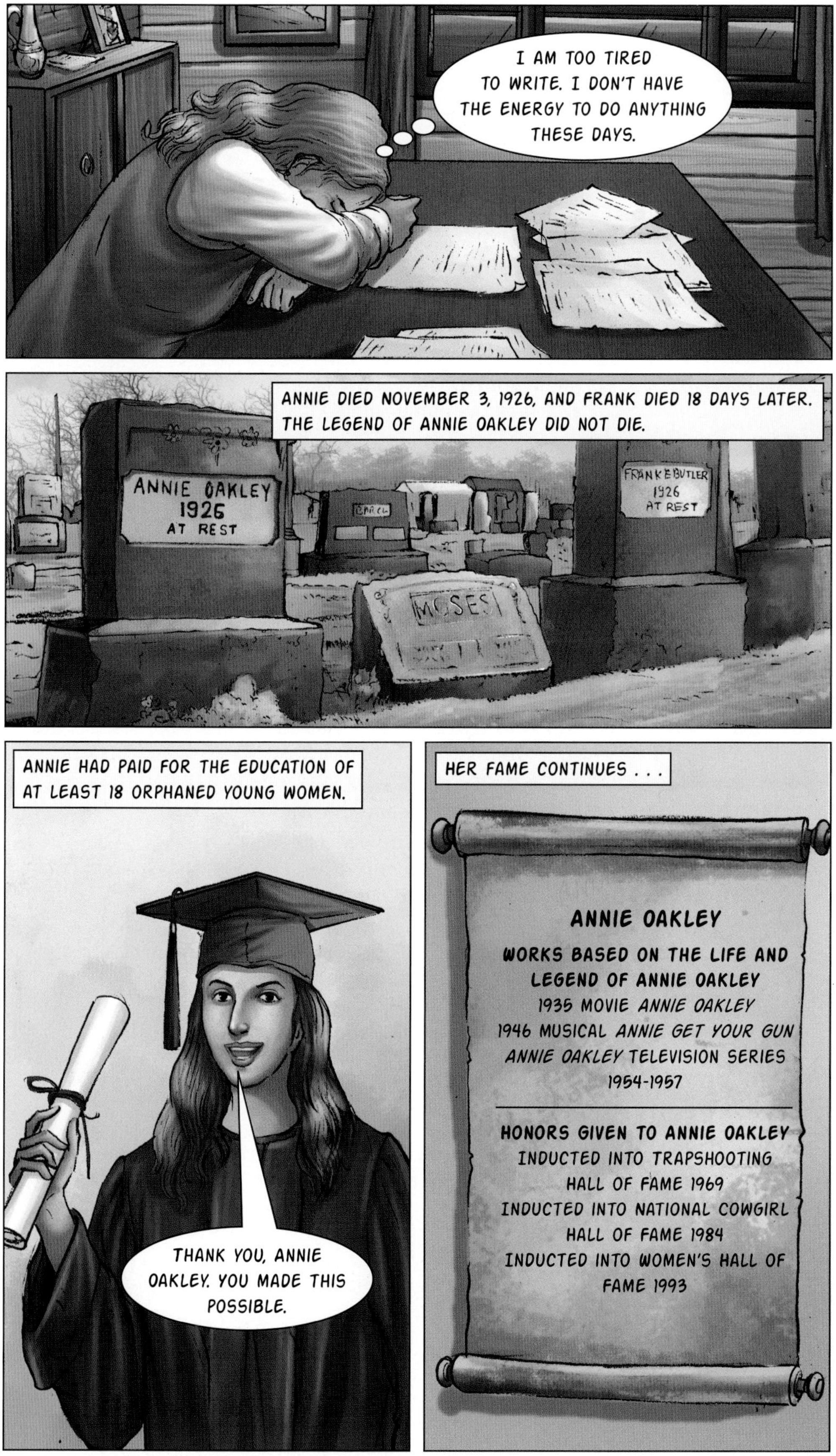
I AM TOO TIRED TO WRITE. I DON'T HAVE THE ENERGY TO DO ANYTHING THESE DAYS.
ANNIE DIED NOVEMBER 3, 1926, AND FRANK DIED 18 DAYS LATER. THE LEGEND OF ANNIE OAKLEY DID NOT DIE.
ANNIE OAKLEY
1926
AT REST
FRANK E BUTLER
1926
AT REST
MOSES
ANNIE HAD PAID FOR THE EDUCATION OF AT LEAST 18 ORPHANED YOUNG WOMEN.
THANK YOU, ANNIE OAKLEY. YOU MADE THIS POSSIBLE.
HER FAME CONTINUES . . .
ANNIE OAKLEY
WORKS BASED ON THE LIFE AND LEGEND OF ANNIE OAKLEY
1935 MOVIE *ANNIE OAKLEY*
1946 MUSICAL *ANNIE GET YOUR GUN*
ANNIE OAKLEY TELEVISION SERIES 1954-1957
HONORS GIVEN TO ANNIE OAKLEY
INDUCTED INTO TRAPSHOOTING HALL OF FAME 1969
INDUCTED INTO NATIONAL COWGIRL HALL OF FAME 1984
INDUCTED INTO WOMEN'S HALL OF FAME 1993

Timeline

August 13, 1860	Phoebe Ann Moses is born in Darke County, Ohio.
November 1875	Annie Moses wins a shooting contest against Frank E. Butler.
August 1876	Annie and Frank Butler are married.
May 1882	Annie appears in a show with Frank for the first time and uses the name Annie Oakley.
March 1884	The couple meets Sitting Bull in St. Paul, Minnesota.
March 1885	Annie and Frank join Buffalo Bill's Wild West show.
June 1885	Sitting Bull joins the Wild West show.
May 1887	The Wild West show opens in London.
1889–1892	The Wild West show tours Europe, and Annie is a superstar.
1901	Annie and Frank leave the Wild West show.
1903–1910	Annie appears in court after a libelous newspaper article is printed about her.
1922	Annie is severely injured in an automobile accident.
November 3, 1926	Annie Oakley dies. Frank Butler dies 18 days later.
1935	A film version of Annie Oakley's life is released.
1946	*Annie Get Your Gun*, a musical written by Rodgers and Hammerstein, opens in New York City.

Glossary

cartridge (KAHR-trij) A tube with a bullet and powder in it that is put inside a gun.

cavalry scout (KA-vul-ree SKOWT) Someone who gathers information about the enemy in battle.

fabricated (FA-brih-kayt-ed) Made something up.

holy man (HOH-lee MAN) A man who is very blessed and has a special role in a group.

kaiser (KY-zer) The title for the rulers of Germany from 1871 to 1918.

moccasins (MAH-kuh-sinz) Native American shoes made of leather and often decorated with beads.

mortgage (MAWR-gij) An agreement to use a building or piece of land as security for a loan. If the loan is not paid back, the lender gets to keep the building or land.

pellets (PEH-luts) Small, round things.

pneumonia (noo-MOH-nyuh) A disease in which the lungs become inflamed and fill with thick liquid.

poorhouse (PUHR-hows) A place for poor people to live.

sharpshooter (SHARP-shoo-ter) A person who is skilled at shooting.

variety shows (vuh-RY-ih-tee SHOHZ) Kinds of entertainment that consist of several different performances that go on one after the other.

World War I (WURLD WOR WUN) The war fought between the Allies and the Central powers from 1914 to 1918.

Index

A

Annie Get Your Gun, 21, 22

B

Battle of the Little Bighorn, 3, 11
Buffalo Bill's Wild West show, 3, 13, 14, 15, 16, 17, 22
Butler, Frank, 3, 8, 9, 12, 21, 22

C

Cincinnati, Ohio, 7
Cody, Buffalo Bill, 3, 12, 13

D

Darke County, Ohio, 4, 22
Darke County Infirmary, 6
Deadwood Dick, 16

E

England, 15, 16

G

Greenville, Ohio, 6, 7

L

Lakota Sioux, 3, 10
Little Bighorn, 3, 11
London, England, 16, 19, 22
Louisville, Kentucky, 12

M

Moses, Jacob, 4
Moses, Susan, 4

N

National Cowgirl Hall of Fame, 21
New Orleans, Louisiana, 12

P

Paris, France, 16
Pony Express, 3

R

"Rifle Queen," 16

S

St. Paul, Minnesota, 10, 22
Salsbury, Nate, 3
Sitting Bull, 3, 10, 11, 22

T

Trapshooting Hall of Fame, 21

V

variety shows, 3
Victoria, Queen of England, 15

W

Wilhelm II, King of Germany, 15, 19
Women's Hall of Fame, 21
World War I, 19

Web Sites

Due to the changing nature of Internet links, PowerKids Press has developed an online list of websites related to the subject of this book. This site is updated regularly. Please use this link to access the link:

www.powerkidslinks.com/jgam/oak/